Smashed Eggs

A Play for 8–11 Year Olds

Phil Porter

A SAMUEL FRENCH ACTING EDITION

SAMUEL
FRENCH

FOUNDED 1830

SAMUELFRENCH-LONDON.CO.UK
SAMUELFRENCH.COM

SMASHED EGGS

Smashed Eggs was commissioned and first produced by Pentabus Theatre. The first performance was at the Arena Theatre in Wolverhampton on 5th February 2002 as part of a national tour. The cast was as follows:

Miranda	Beverley Denim
Titus	Darren Cheek
Angela	Nia Davies

Director and Dramaturg	Dani Parr
Designer	Kate Bunce

Phil Porter won The Children's Award 2003 for *Smashed Eggs*. The Children's Award is made for excellence, inspiration and innovation in children's theatre writing

CHARACTERS

Miranda
Titus
Angela
Mouth Collector

Time—the present

ACT I

Angela's house

Like other houses it has beds, tables, chairs, kitchen stuff and other things

Unlike other houses its walls, ornaments and furniture are meticulously decorated to display in writing one or more of the house rules. There are many house rules. (See pages 51-54)

The stage is in darkness. A tape recording of Angela speaking plays on a tape machine

Angela's Voice Rule number seventy-seven, never put beer into anybody's ear. Rule number seventy-eight, be careful with the ornaments...

A very slight light picks out Titus and Miranda, asleep in their beds

...Rule number seventy-nine, no setting fire to things. Rule number eighty, no juggling with fruit. Rule number eighty-one, no climbing into the refrigerator...

Alarm clocks buzz in strange stereo

...Rule number eighty-two, never scratch your nose in the month of December.

The children silence the alarms and the tapes

Miranda Open your eyes, cabbage for brains.
Titus They're already open, cow features.

Miranda turns a light on

Miranda So they are. I must have mistaken some other ugly thing for your face.
Titus Maybe it was a mirror.

Miranda and Titus tidy their beds away. As they speak they dress

I wish you wouldn't make this room so hot.

Miranda You're the one producing all the hot gas.

Titus My brain is like an actual volcano.

Miranda My brain is twice as hot as yours.

Titus No way.

Miranda Any day. Come to think of it, that is probably because I just had the most amazing dream in the history of sleep.

Titus Only one dream? I had six thousand.

Miranda Get lost, you never.

Titus I did. First I dreamt I was a seahorse, then I dreamt I was an eagle, then I dreamt I was a tiger in a palace in a jungle.

Miranda If you were a tiger they'd kick you out of the jungle.

Titus Actually, I ate the lion and curled up on his throne.

Miranda You'd be kicked out by a group of mice for being such a coward. And anyway, I think a tiger would know which shoe to put on which foot.

Titus looks at his feet and sees his mistake

Titus Tigers don't wear shoes. Ignoramus.

Miranda Mine was a nightmare, so you can shut up.

Titus Every dream's a nightmare for a weakling girl like you.

Miranda Listen who's talking, Mummy's little treasure. It was about a man called The Mouth Collector.

Titus Watch me wet my pants.

Miranda Who hasn't got a mouth on his face.

Titus shrugs a bit nervously. Miranda continues, creeping towards Titus with arms outstretched in a genuinely menacing way

He spends the night-time roaming round and stealing other people's mouths. You can try to run away, but he just keeps catching up. And the white bits in his eyes are red. And his hands are strong as eagle claws. And his home feels like a spider's web. If you ever went there, he'd pick your squashy little mouth off your squashy little face like a magnet off a fridge.

Titus Have you finished? Thank goodness for that, I nearly died of boredom.

Miranda You'll die of something else if you don't check on the Animal and wake your mummy up.

Titus Brush your hair. It looks like a dirty bird's nest.

Titus moves away. Miranda begins to brush the knots from her hair and during the following will move to sit at the table in the breakfast area. Titus goes to where Angela sleeps. He picks up her slippers, brushes the fluff from them and places them on the floor. Beside her bed is a gong. He strikes it gently and speaks slightly wearily

Wake up. It's seven o'clock and all the birds are chirping.

Angela does not wake. Titus stands on one leg and strikes the gong again

Wake up. It's seven o'clock and the owls and the hedgehogs are drifting off to sleep.

Angela Is that my little baby kangaroo?

Titus Please don't call me baby kangaroo.

Angela Have you brushed the fluff from my slippers?

Titus There was no fluff, but I brushed them anyway.

Angela Is my dressing-gown in the warm cupboard?

Titus You saw me put it there last night.

Angela And have you checked on the Animal's health?

Titus Yeah. Still bad. He didn't even squeak when I poked him with the celery.

Angela sits up in bed

Angela Poor old Animal. He seems to get weaker every day.

Titus Dear old Animal.

Angela Illness is a terrible thing. He wouldn't survive ten minutes without his special cage and diet. Poor old Animal.

Titus Dear old Animal. (*He fetches the dressing-gown from the warm cupboard*)

Angela Is Miranda awake?

Titus Awake and behaving like she owns the world.

Angela Titus…

Titus Awake and spouting on as if no-one else existed.

Angela I'm sure she's only trying to be friendly.

Titus That girl is such an irritating stomachache.

Angela Why do you say that?

Titus One, she draws pictures of me when I'm asleep. Two, she picks up earwigs and says they look like me. Three, she hides my toothbrush. And … five, she says that I've got nappy rash. And I never do anything to her.

Angela I thought you two were friends.

Titus Friends do not put spiders in each other's shoes. (*He puts Angela's slippers on her feet*) Why can't she live somewhere else? I preferred it when it was just you, me and Animal.

Angela You know that's not possible.

Titus She's a pain in the absolute neck.

Angela Well, I suppose there might be a bit of room for one or two new rules. We'll make an earwig rule. And we'll make a spider rule. And we'll make a very special rule about not drawing people when they're asleep.

Titus What about my toothbrush?

Angela I must have told you what happens to people who hide toothbrushes. If they do it one too many times, their teeth go yellow and their ears go flaky.

Titus That would serve her completely right.

Angela Be patient with her, Titus. Try to see things through her eyes. She has been through a terrible amount.

Titus That doesn't mean she can...

Angela You like her really.

Titus I'll try not to get too annoyed with her stupid behaviour.

Angela I think we should get breakfast on the boil, don't you?

Angela and Titus enter the breakfast area. Miranda is sitting at the table. It is laid with three plates and three large plastic spoons. There is an egg-holding ornament positioned quite prominently which holds three eggs. Angela looks out of the window

Titus Good morning, Miranda. You look well.

Miranda Really? You look like a bag of dead worms.

Angela Rain is definitely on the way.

Miranda I cooked the breakfast, Angela. It's all in that whacking great saucepan, I had to do something while you two were chatting.

Angela Thank you, Miranda.

Miranda And before you ask, I followed all the rules for cooking breakfast. All forty-six of them.

Angela begins to spoon the peas on to the plates, one spoonful for herself and two for each of the children

Angela A hundred peas for Titus. A hundred peas for Miranda. And fifty peas for me.

Titus Peas remind me of planets.

Miranda Peas remind me of your brain. Green, squashy and not very big.

Angela What a glorious smell.

Miranda It's a shame they taste like balls of mud.

Pause

Why do we always eat peas for breakfast?

Angela Because it's a rule. It's painted on the wall.

Miranda Only because you painted it there. No-one else in the world eats peas for breakfast.

Angela And they suffer the consequences. These peas are why your brains stay round and firm, while the brains of other children turn soft like eggs or dry like toast or sticky like Marmite.

Titus Or gloopy like porridge.

Miranda We could at least have fish, then. What about kippers?

Titus Anyone that eats fish for breakfast grows claws like a crab or a lobster. Sorry, we thought everyone knew that.

Angela Perhaps tomorrow we'll have a change. Treat ourselves by putting in a sprig of mint. But that's enough ungrateful talk for now.

Simultaneously, each drops two sugar cubes into their cup of tea and stirs with a teaspoon. Angela holds her spoon aloft

Rules for breakfast, please.

Titus Breakfast must be eaten with a large plastic spoon.

Miranda Breakfast must consist of peas and only peas.

Titus No making up songs about breakfast.

Miranda No pretending your peas are an army.

Titus No pushing peas about your plate...

Miranda ...Or putting them in pictures, patterns or lines.

Titus No speaking on behalf of peas.

Miranda No banging of plastic spoons.

Titus No spilling.

Miranda No yawning.

Titus No salt without pepper.

Miranda No swallowing without chewing.

Titus No flicking.

Titus puts salt on his peas. Miranda does the same with pepper and Angela with vinegar. They speak all at once

Titus Salt!
Miranda Pepper!
Angela Vinegar!

They slickly switch condiments and do the same thing

Titus Pepper!
Miranda Vinegar!
Angela Salt!

And again

Titus Vinegar!

Miranda Salt!
Angela Pepper!

Angela and Titus rest their little fingers on their noses. Forgetting the next part of the ritual, Miranda is about to eat a spoonful of peas

Hold your horses, eager beaver.

Miranda puts her fingers on her nose

Thank you for the healthy plate of peas I'm about to eat.
Titus For dolphinariums, planetariums, ankles and feet.
Miranda For crumpets and for trumpets and for sheep that bleat.
Angela Thank you for the healthy plate of peas I am about to eat. Thank you for this appetising meal.
Titus For mixing bowls and telegraph poles and the invention of the wheel.
Miranda For oranges and oranges and bits of orange peel.
Angela But most of all, thank you for this appetising meal.

Miranda and Titus set about eating their peas with their plastic spoons. They take mouthfuls simultaneously. Angela cannot see how much they hate the peas

There's nothing I like better than to see a child enjoying a plateful of peas.
Titus They are delicious.
Angela And how lucky we are to have lovely fresh peas, picked from our pretty pea patch, grown in well-drained soil and enriched with well-rotted farmyard manure.

Miranda spits out some peas

Miranda Cow's muck?!
Titus It's all part of the fertilisation process.
Angela They're perfectly clean.
Titus Peas are rich in protein, vitamins, dietary fibre and mineral salts.
Angela That's absolutely correct.
Miranda It's a shame they taste like curled-up woodlice. (*She resumes eating*)
Angela A lot of work goes into the growing of these peas. Digging, watering, picking and protecting them from danger. Protecting them from the cold and from mice and pea moths and bean weevils. Look at you both. Like a pair of perfect peas in a pod. And it's my job to protect you from the dangers of——

Titus Miranda!

Miranda What?

Titus She's pretending her peas are an army!

Miranda Titus!

Titus Look at that!

Miranda I hate you for saying that!

Angela Let me see.

Titus It's as plain as the nose on her face! The big pea is obviously the Sergeant Major and the ones in a line are his regiment! And look! She's even using the pepper as a gunpowder store!

Angela This is extremely serious.

Miranda I don't know what anyone's going on about. (*She scrambles the peas up*)

Titus She's scrambled them up now!

Miranda It was a coincidence, pig face!

Angela I sincerely hope that's true, Miranda. I have told you many times what happens to people pretending their peas are an army. They're sent away to fight in wars, OK, Miranda? Unfamiliar countries and dangerous situations. So don't come crying to me if the Prime Minister knocks on our door——

Miranda It wasn't on purpose.

Angela I sincerely hope that's true.

Miranda They got in a line by themselves.

Angela War is not to be trifled with.

Titus I'd miss you terribly.

Miranda Shut up, baby. I'll get you for that.

Silence but for the munching of peas

Angela... I know that a rule is a rule is a rule. But why are people that pretend their peas are an army sent away to fight in wars?

Angela There's no point in questioning what happens to be.

Miranda But some of it doesn't make sense.

Titus Perhaps your brain just isn't ready.

Miranda Like why do people that try to see into the future grow holly bushes in their heads? Where does the holly even come from? Or why do people that sniff too much go blind? Or why would peanuts make me sick?

Angela You're allergic to peanuts.

Titus You are allergic to peanuts.

Miranda OK, I'm allergic but... There's too many rules when all I want to do is muck about. I feel like I'm drowning in a box...

Titus Somebody climbed out of bed the wrong side.

Miranda Before I moved here I was always——

Angela We mustn't upset ourselves with thinking about the past. I set the rules to make you safe. And to help you to be happy. And because I love you both so much. You understand that, don't you? (*She affectionately puts her hand on Miranda's shoulder*)

Miranda freezes. Angela takes it away again

Miranda I didn't mean to arrange my peas like that.
Angela I'll phone the Prime Minister later on and tell him that it was a false alarm. Now, if we're all finished, I think it's probably time we fed the Animal.

Titus, Miranda and Angela move to the Animal's cage. Ceremoniously, Titus lifts a sheet from the cage to reveal Animal: a mangy and startled but lovable creature. They peer at him gloomily

Miranda Is he still breathing?
Titus Only very slightly. Poor old sick old Animal.
Angela Dear old poor old Animal. I don't suppose you've got much appetite. (*She drops a biscuit into the cage*)
Titus His teeth are getting blunter and his eyes are all tired and blank. They look a bit like tiny scratched black marbles. (*He drops a carrot into the cage*)
Miranda Look, there's a scab on his back in the shape of a violin. And his legs are getting thinner. (*She drops a worm into the cage*)
Angela Your fur used to be so soft to stroke.
Miranda What's the actual matter with him, Angela?
Angela Illness, I'm afraid. A combination of germs and viruses is gumming up his poor little blood. Terrible horrible animal illness. Without the rules I set him and without his special diet he'd have passed away a week or two ago.

They sigh

Titus May I have permission to go and do my painting. I want to paint the stripes on the tiger's face.
Angela Good boy.

Miranda pulls a face at Titus as he leaves

Pause

Miranda May I have permission to go and brush my hair again? It gets all knotted up and stuff dead quickly.

Angela Sit down for a minute.

Miranda Please, Angela, I can feel it knotting up.

Angela Sit down and chat to me for a while.

Miranda sits down on a chair. Angela kneels close in front of her and inspects her face, making Miranda uncomfortable

Miranda It might rain later...

Angela I'm worried about your general well-being, Miranda. I'm worried that your general feelings might not be too cheerful.

Miranda I don't know what you mean.

Angela Your head is like a clenched fist.

Miranda I don't know what you mean.

Angela It's perfectly natural. You've been through a terrible amount. With all that sadness and settling in here, it's perfectly understandable if you feel ... a little anxious day to day.

Miranda I don't feel a little anxious day to day.

Angela Then that's good. But I hope you know that if you ever do feel at all anxious or frightened or peculiar, I hope you know how much I'd like to help.

Miranda nods. Satisfied, Angela stands up and sets about writing or painting something on the side of the washing-up bowl

Miranda I had a dream last night.

Angela Oh, really? Tell me about your dream.

Miranda It was about a man called The Mouth Collector.

Angela What a funny imagination.

Miranda Yeah. Only it wasn't funny, it was horrible. He really loved his wife and baby, but they disappeared. Then a while after that, his mouth disappeared as well. So... In the daytime, he hides in his special secret home with this nasty long-eared rabbit and his other special things. Then at night, he creeps around the world and steals other people's mouths. He picks them off our faces like apples off a tree. And The Mouth Collector's hands are strong and his eyes are red and his arms are twisted and he wears this special secret mask, Angela. And the mask is like... And all the secret things, they look all... I don't remember what they look like but the whole thing was just so creepy. I woke up and my head was like a kettle.

Angela Perhaps you're getting sick.

Miranda I was so scared, I could hardly breathe.

Angela puts her hand on Miranda's forehead

I could hardly move.

Angela My goodness, you are burning up. And look at the shopping bags
under your eyes.
Miranda I don't need medicine, if that's what you're driving at.
Angela Let's see…

Miranda follows the following instructions

Stand up. Stick out your tongue. Close your eyes. Clap. Stick out your
bottom. Put your fingers in your ears. Jump up and down on the spot.

*Miranda does not jump up and down as she cannot hear this instruction.
Angela takes Miranda's fingers from her ears*

It doesn't seem to be anything too serious. Perhaps I'll fetch you some
medicine all the same.
Miranda No, please…
Angela It's better to be safe than it is to be sorry.
Miranda Please, Angela, don't make me drink that stuff.
Angela Titus! Come here my little baby kangaroo!

*Titus enters immediately, wearing a beret and holding a palette and a
paintbrush*

Titus Please don't call me "baby kangaroo". It makes me sound like a baby
kangaroo.
Angela Miranda needs some medicine so I'm going to the chemist. While
I'm gone, it being Saturday, I'd like you two to mop the floor. OK? (*She
gives out mops*) A mop for Titus. And a mop for Miranda. I don't want
squabbles or anyone skiving. Just working together nicely, is that clear?
Titus ⎫ (*together*) Yes.
Miranda ⎭
Angela Good. (*She holds a hand aloft*)

Titus and Miranda put on mackintoshes as they recite

Rules for mopping, please.
Titus No pretending your mop is a snooker cue.
Miranda Mackintoshes must be worn.
Titus No pretending your mop is a microphone.
Miranda No shoving mops into other people's faces.
Titus One scoop of soap per bucket.
Miranda One mop per person.
Titus No scrapping or skidding…

Miranda ...Or pretend sword-fighting with mops.
Angela Good, I should just make it there and back before it starts to rain. Can I trust you both to behave?

Miranda puts her arm around Titus

Miranda Us two? We'll be as good as gold, won't we, old buddy?
Titus I'll make sure she doesn't do anything stupid.

Miranda stamps on Titus's foot. It hurts

Miranda Was that your foot? Sorry, old chum.
Angela And try to get the Animal to eat something while I'm away. His poor little body's getting so thin and weak.
Miranda No problem. Leave everything in our capable hands.
Angela Must change out of these pyjamas.

Angela exits

The children part immediately and Miranda starts mopping the arm that was round Titus's shoulder

Miranda You are such a creepy little whining little bootlicker, Titus. You're always trying to get me into trouble.
Titus It's not my fault if you can't control yourself.
Miranda I wasn't even pretending that my peas were an army. I was pretending my peas were a pop concert.
Titus I'm not an idiot, you know.
Miranda You could have fooled me in that idiot-brained hat.
Titus There's no need to be personal. (*He takes the beret off and strokes it*) As a matter of fact, it makes my painting better.
Miranda Let's just get on with mopping, shall we?

Miranda takes the bowl, that Angela wrote on, off

(*Off*) If we don't finish before she gets back she'll say I've been leading her "little baby kangaroo" astray.
Titus Don't call me baby kangaroo.

Miranda comes back with water in the bucket

Miranda OK, baby kangaroo, you mop over there——
Titus I said don't call me that.

Miranda And I'll mop over here. Baby kangaroo.

They start mopping

Titus I know something that you don't know. A tiger's paw print is actually called a pug mark.
Miranda Who doesn't know that?
Titus And tiger stripes are like fingerprints, because no two tigers have exactly the same pattern. And the heaviest tiger ever weighed was four hundred and sixty-six kilograms. Fourteen times the size of a girl like you.
Miranda There.
Titus What?
Miranda I've written "explosion" on the floor with my mop.

Titus looks

Titus There's no "z" in explosion, pebble brain.
Miranda There's no "z" in shut your mouth either.

They mop

Titus Did you know that a tiger marks out its territory with its own wee? That and other special smells——
Miranda Will you shut up about tigers and mop?!
Titus I am mopping!
Miranda Saturdays are for shopping and mucking about, not for mopping floors and taking medicine. Why mop the floor on a Saturday?
Titus You know exactly why. Saturday's the day when all the insects of the world gather their food. One tiny breadcrumb could attract a plague of cockroaches.
Miranda That's a bag of cobblers.
Titus Is not. She said so when we were fixing the fence.
Miranda I know she said so. I know she said so. But don't you ever imagine for one tiny pea-brained moment that she might be telling lies? Don't you ever wonder for one teeny thick-headed moment whether all these stories might just be a pile of porkies.

Short pause

Titus Why would she make things up?
Miranda Don't ask me. Maybe she's some kind of crackpot.
Titus You shut up.
Miranda Maybe she's some kind of cuckoo-head.

Titus You shut your ungrateful mouth. Maybe you're the cuckoo-head.

Miranda Face it, Titus. The rules make about as much sense as a pig in a rabbit hutch.

Titus You're just grumpy because you've got to drink the medicine. Or is it because you're frightened by your stupid dream which I bet you didn't even have.

Miranda I wasn't frightened by it. Nothing frightens me. (*She begins mopping near the microwave*)

Titus Don't go so near the microwave.

Miranda Why not?

Titus Don't play games, you know why not. The air there makes our stomachs swell and makes our heartbeats weaker.

Miranda Grow a brain. If that was really honestly true they wouldn't even make microwaves.

Titus I seriously believe you should move away…

Miranda The Government would make laws against microwaves. Before I had to come and live in this loony house I stood by microwaves all the time. I virtually lived by microwaves.

Titus Don't lie.

Miranda I'm not the fibber round here. Normal people in the normal world break these rules all the time. So why is it then, when we look out into the street, that we DO NOT see people with swollen stomachs or lobster claws? (*She picks up a household object. On the bottom it says "Don't wear yellow socks."*) Or giant feet from wearing yellow socks?! *Because she makes the whole lot up, that's why!*

Titus If you can't say anything sensible about the world…

Miranda *It's driving me mad!*

Titus You might as well shut your face!

Miranda Deal with it. She lies. She's a strange and messed-up bully that takes everything out on us. Before my entire life went haywire I was allowed to grow my hair and clip my toenails. My mum and dad let me sing in the bath and put posters on the wall and spin in circles until I got dizzy and have a pattern on my duvet and whisper and wink and burp and skip *and have kippers for flipping well breakfast*!!

Titus Then maybe you're lucky they died when they did.

Pause

Miranda takes an egg from the egg holding ornament. She shows it to Titus

Miranda One egg.

Titus What are you doing?

Miranda I'm going to smash it.

Titus Don't be ridiculous. I didn't mean to say that.

Miranda I am, I'm going to smash it.

Titus Stop that now, Miranda. You know exactly what happens when you break an egg. Your body goes all egg-shaped and your skin goes hard and cracks apart.

Miranda I think we should see about that.

Titus begins to slowly creep towards Miranda with his arms outstretched

Titus I'd like you to put the egg down and leave the area in a calm and sensible manner. Gently on the floor now.

Miranda slowly crouches down as if she is planning to place the egg on the floor gently

That's it. Easy as we go. No heroics.

The egg reaches an inch from the floor. Miranda looks up and smiles at Titus, then tosses the egg high into the air. They watch it fall to the floor and smash. Miranda hugs herself and smiles a broad and contented smile

Fabulous, Miranda, that's gone and done it. That's really gone and done it, that has. How very extremely clever you seem to be. I'll just stand and watch you go all egg-shaped, shall I? (*He marches around Miranda, looking for signs of change*) Bye then, Miranda. It was nice knowing you before you went egg-shaped.

Miranda It feels fantastic, Titus. It feels like melted chocolate.

Titus Yeah, until your skin goes hard and cracks apart. What a brilliant decision you just made.

Miranda My skin feels fine.

Titus What a way to go.

Miranda Nothing is happening to my skin and I am not going egg-shaped. She has been stringing us a silly bag of lies.

Titus Maybe it doesn't kick in for a moment or two.

Miranda Face facts, it's all a total sack of trumped-up fairy stories. OK, close your eyes and hold out your hand.

Titus What for?

Miranda What's the matter, gutless chicken, scared of the dark?

Titus makes a show of how fearlessly he can close his eyes and put out his hand. Miranda takes another egg from the holder and puts it in Titus's hand

Are you ready for absolute pleasure?

Titus opens his eyes and fixes a desperate stare on the egg

Titus Take it away.
Miranda It feels like melted chocolate, honestly it does.
Titus You're just scared of being the only egg-shaped one round here.
Miranda You're just scared of what Mummy might say if little baby
  kangaroo broke a little baby rule.
Titus I'm not scared, I'm just bored of the whole thing.
Miranda Don't lie to me. You're dying to feel the crunchy shell crunching
  in your hand like a giant's hand. And all that stringy splidgey egg all oozing
  through your fingers.
Titus Don't you ever shut up?
Miranda If only you had the guts.
Titus Nothing to do with guts in the slightest.
Miranda What a miracle! Miranda still hasn't turned into an egg! Absolutely
  no good reason for Titus not to smash one too. Unless, of course, he's a total
  chicken chicken scared-of-mummy yellow-belly scaredy-cat.
Titus A rule is a rule is a rule is a——
Miranda Pathetic. What a hero!
Titus I am behaving responsibly!
Miranda What a brave tiger! Can't even break an egg! You're nothing like
  a tiger or an eagle. You're just a brainless baby kangaroo that hides in
  Mummy's pouch! A brainless baby——
Titus I'm warning you!
Miranda Pathetic baby kangaroo——
Titus Stop it now!
Miranda Brainless baby kangaroo that hides in Mummy's pouch!

*Titus makes a surprisingly manly screaming sound and crushes the egg in his
hand. Astonished at himself, he drops the shell to the floor and watches as the
strands of egg white hang from his fingers. He puts his clean hand to his face*

Titus My skin's going hard. My glands are swelling. Feel my face, it's
  cracking up!

Miranda grabs Titus's face roughly

Miranda Perfectly normal skin.
Titus Really?
Miranda Honest. So go on then, how did it feel?
Titus It felt… *magnificent!* Melted chocolate.
Miranda Didn't I say?

A distant flash of lightning

Titus When the shell went crack my whole guts went round the bend. Energy bubbles rushing through me. And the crunching noise and the sticky yolk in my paws, it made me feel so... *powerful!*

Miranda places the washing-up bowl on the table. "No hiding of toothbrushes" is on the side of it, freshly painted

Strength from my toes to the tips of my whiskers!

A distant rumble of thunder

What was that noise?!

Miranda Just a bit of thunder. Hey Titus. (*She pours some milk into the washing-up bowl*)

Titus What are you doing?

Miranda I am making one massive mixture.

Titus You are joking me, Miranda.

Miranda I'm going to put milk, peas, toothpaste, beer, sticks, make-up, paint and washing-up liquid in this bowl, and then I'm going to squidge it all about.

Miranda exits purposefully

Titus peers into the bowl

Titus Just because you were right about the egg rule, that doesn't mean that they're all invented. That could just be a blip in the system. And you know what she said would happen if we ever made a mixture. She said our insides would gradually jumble until our hearts were in our heads and our brains were in our chests. That's what she said.

Miranda comes back with toothpaste, sticks, beer and make-up

Miranda That's a sack of twaddle and you know it.

Titus I don't know what I know any more. (*He joins Miranda by the washing-up bowl*)

Miranda I think I'll call it Miranda's Mishmash Gloop. (*She squeezes toothpaste in and adds peas and beer*) A scientific potion for stomach pains and verrucas, stick some washing-up liquid in.

Titus nervously adds washing-up liquid, then feels his chest

That's the boy. (*She adds the following*) And some paint. And some sticks. And some make-up. And a handful of water for good measure. And then

squidge the whole lot up. (*She squidges her Mishmash Gloop about*)
Plunge in and feel it, Titus.
Titus No, thanks.
Miranda Don't be a baby, stick your hands in. (*She grabs Titus's hands and puts them in the mix*)
Titus Miranda! Ooh, that feels good.

They squidge the mixture about, lifting handfuls from the bowl, then watching it gooily plop back in

Miranda I used to make at least one mixture a week. Once I made skin cream with rose petals and mayonnaise and sold it to a neighbour for five pounds.
Titus Get lost, you never.
Miranda It made her look ten years younger and she wasn't that old in the first place. I think I'll open the Animal's cage. (*She wipes her hands on her clothes, goes to the Animal's cage and opens it*) Poor old sick old Animal, locked up all day long. Much rather have some lovely old space to scamper round in, wouldn't you? I'll leave the cage open, you may come and go as you please.
Titus If any harm comes to him, you'll be on the chopping block.
Miranda Don't be such a whingeing little square.
Titus Just a friendly warning.
Miranda Yeah well, one more friendly warning and you'll be on the chopping block and I'll be chopping. (*She starts banging a plastic spoon on the table rhythmically*)

A closer flash of lightning and a louder rumble of thunder

Titus Don't bang plastic spoons, Miranda…

Miranda presses the spoon against Titus's mouth, holds it there a moment, then bangs a few more times and sings

Miranda   Breakfast breakfast
                  Breakfast breakfast
Titus No making up songs about breakfast!

She presses the spoon against his mouth again, holds it there a moment, then resumes banging and singing

Miranda   Breakfast breakfast

Titus is worried about the song at first, but gradually it takes hold of him and he cannot help but join in. They improvise a dance as they sing

Breakfast breakfast
What shall we have for breakfast?
Toasted crumpets and marmalade
Stick it all in my mouth mouth mouth mouth

Breakfast. Breakfast.
What shall we have for breakfast?
Smoked kippers and yoghurt and stuff
Stuff it all in my gob gob gob gob

Miranda picks up a mop with her spare hand and uses it like a microphone

	Breakfast. Breakfast.
	What do you want for your breakfast? (*She puts the microphone mop in Titus's direction*)
Titus	Sausages,sausages,sausages
	And a runny fried egg and a cup of tea
Miranda	A runny fried egg and a cup of tea (*She burps*)
Titus	A runny fried egg and a cup of tea (*He burps*)
Titus & Miranda	A runny fried egg and a cup of tea (*They burp*)
	Breakfast breakfast
	What shall we have for breakfast?
Miranda	Cereal with nuts and stuff
Titus	Beans on toast with mushrooms in
Miranda	Pancakes with bananas on
Titus	Bread with bits of chocolate in
	All crammed in my mouth mouth mouth mouth
Titus & Miranda	Mouth mouth mouth mouth
	Mouth mouth mouth mouth
	Mouth mouth mouth mouth
Miranda	All through the wintertime
	She made them just eat peas
Titus	Then she went away and left us here
	And we very soon agreed
Titus & Miranda	*We'll have a very fine breakfast indeed*

Titus takes a handful of Mishmash Gloop

Miranda	Breakfast breakfast
	Mouth mouth mouth mouth
	Mouth mouth mouth mouth
	Breakfast...

Titus throws the Gloop and it splats on Miranda

I'll get you for that. I'll splat you for that. (*She gets a handful and throws it at Titus*)

A Gloop battle ensues. Miranda gains the upper hand and Titus scarpers. She chases him as he darts about the room and under the table. For a moment he hides and she loses him

I know exactly where you are.

Titus pops up and throws a banana at Miranda. The chase begins again and she has nearly caught him when he grabs a mop. A closer flash of lightning

Titus On guard, foolish challenger!

Miranda grabs the other mop

Miranda On guard, potato-brained warrior!

A louder rumble of thunder and the sound of rain outside begins

Titus I have slain a thousand dragons with the mop you see before you. I don't imagine a girl will prove too difficult. (*He swings his mop twice*)

Miranda defends well

Miranda Think again, foolish mop-swinger! I'm just as strong as any boy and twenty times more nimble.
Titus As nimble as a hippo, perhaps! (*He swings his mop twice more*)

Again Miranda defends well

Miranda Did a feather brush my sword?!
Titus Indeed! A feather of death!

Miranda goes on the attack and Titus defends

Indeed you are as nimble as a kitten. But how can you cope with the strength of a tiger?! (*He lunges with his mop*)

Miranda dodges and grabs the other end of it. They swing themselves once round clockwise making a "whoa" sound, then once round anti-clockwise making an "aaah" sound

Miranda I'm going to play some music and dance.
Titus No way am I dancing.
Miranda Please your stupid self.

She lets go of the mop, causing Titus to fall on his bum

Whoops-a-daisy!

Miranda goes off

Titus picks himself up, goes to the table and uses his mop like a snooker cue to poke something

(*Off*) Your mum's music is such a sack of junk. Who plays records any more?

Classical music begins to play loudly

Miranda comes back

Titus begins to scatter handfuls of peas in a ceremonious way. With great seriousness, Miranda begins dancing in a strange half-ballet-half-girl-band style, trying to account for every mood and twist in the music. A closer flash of lightning and a louder rumble of thunder. As she dances, she makes even more mess, knocking stools over and messing up anything else around. Titus throws peas everywhere. He then tires of pea throwing and decides to conduct the music. Seamlessly he changes from conducting the music to copying Miranda's dance routine. A closer flash of lightning and a louder rumble of thunder. To Miranda's increasing annoyance, they keep bumping into each other

Get off, you're spoiling it! (*She wrestles Titus to the ground then straightens her clothes and continues the routine*)

A closer flash of lightning and a louder rumble of thunder. Titus crawls back to the table, pretending to be a caterpillar. He climbs on to it and stirs the Gloop with his mop. A flash of lightning very nearby and a very loud rumble of thunder. He picks out a stick and conducts. He sees the bottle of beer on the table and picks it up

As he swigs it, Angela walks into the room. She is wet from the rain. She holds a bottle of medicine. She is utterly, utterly horrified at what she sees. She screams a peculiar scream

There is an almighty flash and crash as lightning strikes the house. The light-bulbs blow and the offstage record player explodes. In the dim, eclipse-like light, Miranda runs at Angela and pushes her over

YOU LIIIAAAR!

Miranda stands over Angela for a short moment, then leaves

Angela Miranda, come back!

Pause

Titus. Help me. Give me your hand.

Titus does not move

Titus? Titus? Baby Kangaroo?

Titus leaves

Please come back. Both of you. It really isn't safe. Please... Please! You're my pair of perfect peas in a pod. (*She crawls to the table. She mumbles as she crawls*) Oh, my goodness... Something terrible will happen... I know it will... I know it will... Please don't let something terrible happen... (*She uses the table to get herself back on her feet. She lights the candle*) You understand, don't you, Animal? I only make the rules to be kind. Only to protect you all from danger. (*She holds the candle up to the cage*) You wouldn't survive ten minutes without your special cage and diet, would you, Animal? Animal, where are you?

End of Act I

ACT II

SCENE 1

Twilight hangs and shadows loom across a grassless patch of land on the edge of a wood quite far from anywhere

Four tree stumps, irregularly spaced, poke out of the ground. A pile of blackened twigs and ash, surrounded by a circle of stones and boulders, sits in the centre of this eerie place. Some branches and a grimy black plastic sheet are strewn across the ground. Weird sounds and nasty shadows inhabit this place

Angela enters, looks around and feels a chill run down her spine. She calls out and her voice echoes creepily

Angela Titus. Miranda. Please come out if you're hiding. This place, it really doesn't feel safe. You caught me by surprise, that's all. Please come out. You're my pair of perfect peas in a pod...

Short pause

I never told you what happens to children that run away. It's a terrible thing. Their bodies slowly turn into shadows. And not just normal shadows. Terribly long, cold, sad ones. And bats and field-mice live inside their heads. And their knees make noises like creaking windmills. And their eyeballs turn to ice-blocks and their tongues go hard and black. But that's only if they stay out all night. Please come home. Come home and we'll forget you ever did it.

Angela moves on

An owl hoots. Very faintly, an unseen woman sings in a sad and distant way. A mysterious shadow passes across the stage

Titus and Miranda walk into the space. Titus is very scared

Titus What was that?
Miranda What?

Titus I saw something move.

Miranda Probably a shadow of a branch. Where are we?

Titus Wherever it is, it's making my blood freeze.

Miranda Some tiger you'd make.

Titus Get lost, Miranda, even a tiger would have found that forest spooky.
And this place is hardly any better. My spine feels like an icicle.

Miranda stops walking and Titus walks round in circles

Miranda It's getting really dark ...

Titus Don't remind me!

Miranda Maybe we should set up camp for the night.

Titus Is that some kind of joke? I would much rather keep walking if it's all
the same to you. Every time I stop it's like a ghost walks through my body.

Miranda But we can't keep walking forever. My feet are getting blisters and
we need to save our energy.

Titus If we just keep going until morning we'll be——

Miranda Stand still, Titus!

Titus stands still

I've made a decision and we're setting up camp here. I am the oldest.

Titus Here?

Miranda It's perfect.

Titus It's the creepiest place in the universe.

Miranda But there's stumps to sit on, look. And a fireplace for fires. And
the view across the field is fairly...

Titus Spine-chilling. I am not being funny, but the air round here is weirdly
cold and there is something about these shadows——

Miranda Stop being such a thick-headed baby.

Titus OK, then, what if someone still lives here? And what if they find us
on their patch of ground?

Miranda Nobody lives here.

Titus Well, someone lit a fire. (*He begins walking round in circles again*)

Miranda Years ago, probably. We'll stay here for tonight, OK? If in the
morning it still doesn't feel like home, we'll go and find somewhere else.
If we decide we like it, we can stay forever.

Titus I'd rather live in Dracula's castle.

Miranda You're making me dizzy, Titus. Why don't you lie down and have
a rest. Take a few deep breaths.

Titus What, sleep down there with wolves and weasels sniffing round my
feet? And spiders lowering themselves on to my face? You're even madder
than I thought.

Miranda Why don't you stick up a tent, then?

Titus stops

Titus If I had a tent to stick up that's exactly what I'd do.
Miranda Build one then. Build one with the stuff that's lying round.
Titus If you can tell me how to build a tent with the stuff in this complete empty nightmare of a place, I'll give you a million pounds.
Miranda OK. There's a plastic sheet down there. And some branches and some stones. And there was a traffic cone a little way back. Stick the stick in the ground and the sheet on top, prop it up with the cone and weight it down with the stones.
Titus You know I haven't got a million pounds.

Titus goes to fetch the traffic cone

(*As he goes*) If you're so clever, I don't know why you can't build it.
Miranda I'm not the kangaroo that wants a tent. I'm at my happiest gazing up at the stars.

Now alone, Miranda lets her guard down slightly. She picks up a couple of stones and lobs them at a tree stump. The faint singing voice is heard again, apparently coming from the tree stump. Puzzled and scared, Miranda moves towards the tree stump. The singing fades away

Titus returns with a traffic cone

Was that you singing?
Titus What have I got to sing about?
Miranda I thought I heard a voice. It was creepy.

Titus begins to build the tent

Hey Titus, maybe this place is haunted.
Titus Shut your stupid mouth.
Miranda Maybe a man-eating monster lives here. Or the ghost of The Lady In White. Have you heard of The Lady In White?
Titus You think you're hilarious but you're actually extremely boring——
Miranda She was drowned in the lake on a freezing night by her evil cowardly husband. Now she haunts all cowards for revenge, attacking them when they least expect it.
Titus You'd better watch out, then.
Miranda Or this could be the home of the vicious one-legged zombie. (*She begins to hop around with arms outstretched zombie-style*) He died of shock when his leg fell off and he turned into a zombie. Now he hops

around the world with his eyes wide open and his arms stretched out, and
he zombifies the people that he meets.

Titus My head is actually aching with boredom.

Miranda Or the spirit of Seven-Eyed Jack. Or The Phantom Body Snatcher!
Or the ghost that has the head of a goat but the body of a school teacher!
This could be where she lives——

Titus You're not being funny so you might as well belt your mouth up!

Miranda Or The Mouth Collector from my dream.

Titus finishes the tent. It is not very good

Titus There, I've finished. What do you think?

*Miranda inspects the tent from a variety of angles. She moves one of the
stones a fraction and steps back to admire her handiwork*

Miranda Perfect. What a team. Now, let's sit down and enjoy our new life.

They sit. Long pause

Titus Aren't you even slightly scared, Miranda?

Miranda Don't be such a weakling, there's nothing to be scared of.

Long pause

This is fun.

Titus It's about as much fun as an ear infection.

Miranda Don't be so negative.

Titus An ear infection on a windy day.

Pause

And much less safe.

Miranda Are you hungry?

Titus I could eat a rhinoceros.

Miranda I've got a biscuit.

Titus Why didn't you say before?

Miranda Do you want half or not? (*She takes a foil-wrapped biscuit from
somewhere on her person*) I thought we could have it as a midnight feast,
but all that walking made me dead hungry.

Titus Hurry up. (*He holds out his hand*)

Miranda looks into the foil and is disappointed

Miranda Oh. (*She pours some biscuit crumbs into Titus's hand*) It must have
got crushed when I slipped on that dead hedgehog.

Titus brushes his hands clean disdainfully and sulks

Cheer up. You look like you've swallowed a miserable frog.

Titus No food, no comfortable furniture. Ghosts. No radiators…

Miranda No exact bedtime, no mopping, no dusting, no watering the pea
patch or speaking French on Tuesdays. No-one telling you when you can
paint. If Titus wants to paint a picture, Titus paints a flipping picture!

Titus I didn't even bring any brushes.

Miranda We can buy brushes.

Titus What with?

Miranda Come on, don't be like that. This is freedom at last. And it might
take a little tiny bit of getting used to, but freedom is honestly a massive
sack of fun.

Titus Is it?

Miranda Think how much fun we were having before Old Strict Knickers
came back. It's going to be like that all the time. There's only one rule in
this joint and that's that there are no rules. OK?

Titus This joint makes me feel sick.

Miranda Never mind that, what shall we do first?

Titus I don't know.

Miranda You choose. Anything.

Titus I suppose we could run about.

Miranda That is a brilliant idea.

Miranda jumps up and helps a less enthusiastic Titus to his feet

OK then, let's run over there!

They run to the place and stop

Over there now!

With a bit less enthusiasm, they run to the place and stop. Short pause

Back over there?

*They jog half-heartedly back to their starting place. Pause as they contemplate
despair*

Titus We could have a swordfight like before if we had mops.

Miranda sees a branch on the ground and grabs it

Miranda On guard, potato-brained warrior.

Titus grabs one too

Titus On guard, foolish challenger. I've slain a thousand dragons with the branch you see before you. Prepare for something ferocious.
Miranda "I don't imagine a girl will prove too difficult."
Titus What?
Miranda That's what you say.
Titus I was doing it different.
Miranda Well, do it the same!
Titus OK. I don't imagine a girl will prove too difficult. (*He swings his branch twice*)

Miranda defends well

Miranda Think again, foolish branch-swinger! I'm just as strong as any boy and twenty times more nimble.
Titus As nimble as … an elephant, perhaps!
Miranda No.
Titus A cow perhaps!
Miranda No.
Titus A … badger perhaps?
Miranda Hippo!
Titus Sorry. Hippo perhaps! (*He swings his branch twice more*)

Miranda again defends well

Miranda Did a feather brush my sword?!
Titus A feather?
Miranda A feather of death! (*She goes on a ferocious attack*)

Titus defends

Titus I know this bit. You are as nimble as a tiger. But how can you cope with the strength of a kitten?!
Miranda The other way around!

Baffled, Titus turns to face the other way

Titus You are as nimble as a tiger. But how can you cope——

Miranda This is the worst swordfight in history!! (*She throws her branch down in frustration*)

Titus I can't concentrate. This place——

Miranda What have you got in your head?! A pickled onion?!

Titus No.

Miranda A dead gerbil?!

Titus Let's just do something else.

Miranda All right. All right, let's smash up the tent. Let's trample this idiotic tent up!

Titus We can't. We'll have nowhere——

Miranda begins to trample. Titus tries to stop her

Miranda We can do whatever we like——

Titus Miranda——

Miranda No flipping rules if I remember correctly.

Titus Miranda! Have your brains fallen out or something?! Miranda!

Miranda finishes trampling

Miranda There.

Titus That is the dimmest, dumbest, thickest, stupidest thing that anybody ever did in the history of mankind. We've got nowhere to sleep.

Miranda I don't terribly care.

Titus There could be man-eating monsters round here. And there could be ghosts. And there could be fierce animals. That is not my cup of tea.

Miranda Your voice is like a squeaky blackboard.

Titus Never smash our shared things up again, all right?!

Miranda All right!

Titus That's a rule!

Miranda Fine!

Titus The sheet's all torn now. Go and find another.

Miranda leaves

Thunder rumbles

SCENE 2

Angela walks along a hill path, carrying a rucksack. Nearby, Animal sits on a rock

Angela And your eyebrows grow right round your face. And your fingers turn bright blue. And every time you close your eyes, you see witches and goblins and gravestones and... (*Exhausted, Angela stops, to look out across the town*) Please come home. The world's not safe and I think a storm's brewing up. And remember, it's Saturday night. That means a slice of banana cake for tea. Please come home. (*She decides to rest on the rock. She sits on Animal*)

Animal squeaks. Angela jumps up and sees him

Animal? Is that you? (*She looks closer*) The scab in the shape of a violin! It is you! You squeaked! I thought without your cage that you'd be dead within an hour. Without your heating lamp and special diet. Your teeth, they're sharp again. Your eyes are like emeralds. And the strength of your legs! What have you been eating?! (*She picks up Animal and holds him close to her face*) I've been stupid, Animal. I've been stupid, haven't I?

SCENE 3

The camp is under siege from a thunderstorm. It is so dark that nothing can be seen, but howling wind, lashing rain, rumbling thunder and screaming Titus can be heard

Titus Miranda! Miranda! We're being blown away!

Flashes of lightning reveal Titus in various scenarios of windswept panic. Suddenly, the storm subsides and some light falls on the scene. Titus is wet, baffled and bedraggled. The sound of the singing woman returns

Hallo? (*He looks around in search of the sound's source, eventually realizing that it comes from one of the tree stumps. Tentatively, he approaches the stump*) Hallo? Are you trapped in there? Is there anything I can do to help? I've got a tool box at home but... Please stop singing. (*He knocks on the stump*)

The singing gets louder

Please stop, my nerves are jangling. There's nothing I can do.

The singing gets louder. Titus knocks on the stump

I don't understand what you want! Just stop it! Please stop! (*He bangs hard on the top of the stump*)

The stump flips open to reveal a secret compartment. The singing becomes louder and unmuffled. Titus peers inside. Terrified but curious, he reaches into the stump and takes out a picture frame. The singing fades away as he looks at the picture. He speaks into it

Hallo?

A female figure, swathed all in white, walks silently into the space, unseen by Titus. She stretches a hand out towards Titus in a mysterious and menacing way

A crow caws. Titus feels the presence of the swathed figure. He turns slowly to face her. She looks at him. He is gripped with fear

The Lady In White.

Suddenly, she rushes at Titus with her arms outstretched. He dodges her first lunge, but she soon catches him

There must be some mistake! *Let go of me!!* (*He breaks free and grabs a branch. He swipes the branch at her twice*)

She evades it skilfully. He takes an almighty third swing, misses again and overbalances. While he is face-down on the ground, she hides. He gets up and can't see her

I know you're still here, I can hear you breathing. Miranda will be back in a minute and she'll... Miranda! Come back here a minute! *Please!*

The swathed figure creeps out from her hiding place, still unseen by Titus

There's something that I really need some help with!

She pounces on Titus and pins him to the ground. He whimpers and wails pathetically

I'm not a coward, so please don't hurt me. Please, I'm begging you, please.

She begins to laugh

Miranda! *Help!* It's The Lady in white! *It's the Lady in White!*

Continuing to laugh, The Lady In White uncovers her face to reveal her true identity: it is Miranda. Miranda laughs as Titus realizes her trick

You cruel idiot.

Miranda (*mocking*) I'm not a coward so please don't hurt me.

Titus That is the most spiteful thing——

Miranda What a tiger!

Titus If you think that's funny you need your brain looking into.

Miranda It was only a bit of spooking around.

Titus I thought I was dead. My whole life flashed up in front of me.

Miranda You put up a decent enough fight for a baby. I don't know why you're so upset.

Titus Because things are spooky enough without us spooking each other around! OK?!

Miranda OK.

Titus No more spooking about!

Miranda All right.

Titus Because I'm telling you, things are getting pretty flipping mind-boggling round here. (*He points out the picture frame*) Pictures in picture frames...

Miranda Where did that come from?

Titus You won't believe me but it came from that tree stump.

Miranda Get lost.

Titus Honestly.

Miranda picks up the picture and looks at it. It makes her smile and be sad

Miranda Look at the picture. The baby's eyes are bluer than anything. And the Mummy's smile. They all look so completely...

The sound of a baby crying comes from a different tree stump

Can you hear a baby crying?

Titus That's what I'm telling you. It's coming from a tree stump. While you were away I heard a woman. She was singing to herself in the tree stump.

Miranda I heard a woman singing.

Titus So I went straight up and I barged on the stump and that's where I found the picture frame.

Miranda The stump just opened up?

Titus Yes. When I banged it.

They listen to the baby crying

Miranda It's coming from that one. (*She puts the frame down lovingly on its stump*)

They creep towards the crying stump

Open it, then.

In expert fashion, Titus puts his ear close to the top of the stump and listens to the hollow sound as he taps it lightly with two fingers. He then leans back and whacks it, flipping it open. The baby's crying becomes louder and clearer

Is there a baby?
Titus It's a doll.
Miranda Dolls don't cry like that. What kind of person leaves a baby in a tree stump?
Titus No, it's a doll. (*He pulls the doll from the tree stump*)

It is peculiar and beautiful, with a dark and shiny head, across which creeping vines are painted

How can we make it stop?
Miranda Hold her closer and pat her back. Poor thing, she's crying her lungs out.

Uncomfortably, Titus holds the doll closer and pats her back

Titus It doesn't feel like a living person. Just like a doll but softer.
Miranda She smells all sweet like a baby though. She smells like sweet milk.
Titus It won't stop crying. My nerves are getting tense.
Miranda You're not doing it properly. Give her to me.

Titus passes the doll to Miranda

Titus Things are getting dead, dead strange.
Miranda I know.
Titus Maybe it's a sign. Maybe we should go back.
Miranda I think she's cold. I think we should wrap her in the sheet. Lay it out flat.

Titus lays the sheet out flat and Miranda places the doll down. As they wrap her up…

No need to cry, little one. You'll be as warm as toast. Make sure her feet are covered. (*She picks up the wrapped doll*)

The crying stops

Titus What a relief! Right, I think we should probably go now. One more minute in this place——

Miranda Go? We haven't even looked in the other two stumps.
Titus I think we should go all the same. It could be anything stuck in those stumps.
Miranda Exactly. Like treasure or secrets or food for the baby.
Titus It's not a baby, it's a scary doll! It doesn't have a stomach!

Short pause

Miranda We should still look. If we don't look we'll spend the rest of our lives wondering.
Titus If we have lives.
Miranda Do you really want to walk back through the forest?

Short pause

Titus OK, but you bang it. I'm standing well back.
Miranda OK. Hold the baby.
Titus It's a doll.
Miranda Carefully, she's asleep. (*She passes the doll to Titus and approaches the third tree stump*) No noises this time. (*She bangs the top of the stump*)

It flips open and she looks in

I can't see anything. Shall I put my hand in?
Titus Your choice.

Nervously, Miranda puts her hand in. She pulls out a miniature pair of striped pyjamas on a hanger

Miranda Those are the smallest pyjamas I have ever seen. (*She gently puts the pyjamas by the picture frame. She looks at the picture again*)
Titus Is that it? A tiny pair of pyjamas?
Miranda There might have been something else.
Titus Take this thing off me.
Miranda The dad's hands are five times the size of the baby's.
Titus This thing doesn't even have proper hands. (*He passes the doll over to Miranda*)

She holds the doll, still looking at the picture. Titus goes to the second stump and pulls out a stack of masks. He looks at them. One is oddly similar to the doll with a haunting design that incorporates tiger stripes

Masks. Look at this mask, Miranda. Tiger stripes. It's the strangest, most amazing... (*He gives in to his desire to wear it*) Look at me in the mask.

It smells like something dead. (*He looks back into the stump*) There's more! There's a whole stack! (*He pulls a stack of similar masks from the stump and looks at a couple*)

They all have different mouths. Miranda turns to look at Titus. Horror and confusion spread across her face

Miranda Titus.
Titus What?
Miranda I've seen it before.
Titus What?
Miranda That mask you're wearing, I know I have! It's so familiar, it makes me feel sick!
Titus Don't lie, where would you have seen——
Miranda I don't know! I'm racking my brains but I can't remember!
Titus Maybe it's imagination.
Miranda Whatever it is, it's making my blood cold.
Titus You're making my blood freeze.

Miranda lays the baby down and looks at the masks, racking her brains. Titus tries to take the mask off

Oh, no. You are joking. It's stuck on my head, Miranda. The stinking thing's stuck on my head. I can't spend the rest of my life like this! It won't ... *budge*!

Miranda takes two green apples from the tree stump

Miranda Fresh apples.
Titus What?!
Miranda Two fresh green apples in the stump.
Titus Somehow I've lost my flipping appetite!
Miranda Someone still lives here, Titus. They've only just been left here. Otherwise, they'd be rotten. That is someone's fireplace and these are someone's things!

Pause

Titus Mustn't jump to conclusions.
Miranda It's true.

Pause

Titus We're going. Even through the forest——

Miranda We are not going anywhere——
Titus This is not a game——
Miranda If this idiot wants to live here, he can fight us for it. Titus?
Titus If we run as fast as we can——
Miranda I am not running anywhere. I am sick to my guts of moving round
  from place to place.
Titus It could be some kind of murderer.
Miranda What kind of murderer keeps pictures in frames?! Listen, Titus,
  if those are his pyjamas we have nothing to be frightened of, do we? We'll
  stay and fight.

Pause

Titus We don't even know what's in the fourth stump yet. It might be full
  of blood and bones.
Miranda OK. Open it.
Titus Why me?
Miranda You're better at it.

Titus moves to the fourth stump

Titus *This thing on my head!*
Miranda We'll sort it out later.

*Titus bangs on the top of the stump but nothing happens. He bangs again and
nothing happens. He sees that this stump is different and removes the entire
top section of the stump to reveal a peculiar rabbit, similar in some ways to
Animal and in other ways to the doll and the mask, with ears three feet long.
Titus laughs a nervous, hysterical laugh*

  It's not funny.
Titus Look at the size of them!
Miranda No, Titus…
Titus I bet it can hear Australia!
Miranda Put it back!
Titus What?
Miranda I said put it back!

Titus replaces the top part of the stump

Titus Who's the chicken now? It's only a rabbit.
Miranda That rabbit is the rabbit of The Mouth Collector.
Titus What?

Miranda The mouth-stealing man in my dreams. That is his rabbit and those
 are his special masks. That's his family in the picture. His wife and baby
 that disappeared. This must be his secret home!

Titus We are going.

Miranda No.

Titus I value my mouth, Miranda!

Miranda I know we can beat him.

Titus I don't even want to see him.

Miranda You can't run away from The Mouth Collector! He just keeps
 catching up! I'll stay and guard. Go and find some decent weapons.
 Something with a spike. (*She shakes Titus by the shoulders*) Come on,
 Titus, be brave.

Titus leaves, wrapping himself in the black sheet

Miranda stands on guard. A rumble of thunder. She hears a twig snap

 Is there anybody there? Anybody?

The doll lets out a little cry. Miranda comforts it without picking it up

 It's OK, baby. It's OK, little one.

*The doll stops crying. Miranda hears another noise. She moves away from
the doll*

 Is there anybody there?

*The Mouth Collector walks into the space. He wears a mask similar to the
one stuck on Titus's head, and similar clothes. Miranda mistakes him for
Titus*

 Titus! You haven't got anything! You haven't even looked!

*Frantic, furious and deeply ashamed, The Mouth Collector goes to his
special things. He hugs the doll tightly, then puts the scattered masks and the
pyjamas back into stumps*

 Titus, what are you doing? Stop it. We need weapons. Leave that stuff
 alone! We need weapons! *This is a state of emergency!*

Titus comes back

Titus I can't find anything. We'll have to use branches.

Miranda screams. The Mouth Collector looks at Miranda

Miranda The Mouth Collector.

Very slowly, The Mouth Collector begins to move towards Miranda with violent intent, his twisted arms outstretched. Slowly, petrified, never looking away, she starts to retreat. Like a predator cornering its prey, he manoeuvres her around the space until she is standing with Titus, then begins to encroach

His eyes.
Titus Oh, my flipping...
Miranda And his hands!
Titus Make him stop.
Miranda I think he wants my mouth, Titus. I think he almost definitely wants my mouth. He's getting closer.
Titus Leave it to me. I'll scare him away.
Miranda Don't be silly, Titus——
Titus I said leave it to me!

Short pause as The Mouth Collector gets closer. Titus lets out a yell

Miranda He's still getting closer.

Titus lets out a stronger yell

Careful, Titus——

Titus screams and runs at The Mouth Collector. The Mouth Collector catches him by the neck

Titus You don't frighten me, Mouth Collector. Creeping up on people at night... You're more of a coward than me! I know your wife and baby disappeared, but people's mouths belong on people's faces, Mouth Collector. And no amount of stolen mouths will ever bring them back. So why don't you just leave us alone?
Miranda He's not shifting.
Titus I said go away.
Miranda Get lost! Go away!
Titus Go away before I get angry!

Pause

Leave us alone!!

Miranda Get out of our home!!
Titus *Why don't you just leave us alone*!!

The Mouth Collector hurls Titus to one side, and rushes at Miranda

Cover your mouth!

Miranda covers her mouth with her hands but The Mouth Collector grabs her wrists to prise them away

Miranda I can't hold on! His hands are too strong!!

The doll cries. The Mouth Collector freezes for a moment, then rushes to the doll, gathers it in his arms and runs away. Titus dashes across to Miranda

Titus Miranda! Are you OK?
Miranda So strong, I could hardly move! Thanks, Titus, you were dead
    brave.
Titus Really?
Miranda Yeah, brave as a tiger.
Titus Do you think he'll come back?
Miranda Of course he will. He just didn't want the baby here.
Titus Let's get running then, before it's too late.
Miranda We can't! He'll just keep catching up! We'll stay here——
Titus Miranda, are you mad?! He nearly took your mouth!!
Miranda Too late.
Titus What?

Miranda points

Miranda In the distance.
Titus Oh, no. Maybe it's just a shadow from those branches.
Miranda It's coming this way and it's got a head and legs.
Titus Probably a passer-by.
Miranda It's him. He's coming back. If we hide down by that tree stump,
    when he comes we can rush at him together.
Titus I feel sick.

They hide

He looks pretty angry. And he's carrying a bag.
Miranda It's probably full of snakes or something.
Titus Probably snakes with fangs like knives!

Miranda Or spears tipped with poison!
Titus Shhhh!

They wait in nervous silence for a few seconds. Miranda counts down from three with her fingers

A hooded figure walks into the space

Titus and Miranda scream, run and push the intruder over. The hood falls away to reveal Angela. Animal's head is poking out of the top of her backpack, unharmed

Miranda Angela?
Angela Miranda!
Titus Mum?
Angela Titus, is that you?
Titus It's stuck on my head. I can't get it off.
Angela Are you both OK?
Titus We thought you were The Mouth Collector.
Angela Oh, thank goodness. Thank goodness you're both safe.
Titus Only just.
Angela Let's just all go home, shall we? There's going to be another thunderstorm.
Titus Yeah, come on, Miranda.
Miranda No way am I going back to your weirdo house.
Angela Please, Miranda, it's just not safe——
Miranda Don't even try and persuade me.
Angela I know you're upset, but things can change.
Titus He'll be back any second!
Angela We can sit down and talk. When I found Animal——
Miranda Who wants to talk to a massive stupid cheat?!
Angela When I found Animal——
Miranda Shut up.
Titus Please!
Angela I'll make things different.
Miranda Yeah, with more bags of lies.
Titus So many lies, Mum.
Angela If you give me a chance——
Miranda I've given you a million chances!
Angela But I promise.
Miranda Your promises count for about as much as a dead monkey round here! Because listen to me, all right. I am sick to absolute death of your stupid way of doing things. I am not a pea and I am not perfect and I do not

need someone locking me up in a box! I hate your house and I hate your way of doing things, so why don't you leave me alone?! Go on, get lost, you don't even flipping well like me! Making me do things I hate for the fun of it. Telling me lies for the fun of it. So just get out of my home! (*She throws an apple at Angela*) Go, I said! Can't you hear me?! (*She throws a mask*) Get out of my home, I said! (*She picks up the picture frame to throw*) I hate your rules and I hate your lies and I hate... (*She wants to say "you" and throw the picture frame but can't. She shows Angela the picture*) Why can't things be more like the picture? My life used to be good like the picture. Why can't things be more like the picture? (*She lies face down on the floor, exhausted and tearful, clutching the picture*)

Angela and Titus curl on top of her comfortingly. They are like a snug family of cats

Angela Let's try, then. Let's try for that.

Pause

Titus Maybe we should go now, Miranda.

They uncurl and Angela helps Miranda up

Angela Let's get this one home, shall we? Into the warm. Titus, would you like to carry Animal?

Titus looks down at the rucksack

Angela and Miranda head off

Titus What's he doing out of his cage? Hey Mum, have you seen his fur?! And his eyes don't look scratched up any more. The illness must have gone! Come on, old boy. (*He puts the rucksack on his back*) Flip me, he weighs a ton.

Titus leaves

(*Going off*) Hey Mum, I was dead brave earlier...

Short pause

The Mouth Collector rushes into the space, his arms outstretched, ready to tear their mouths away. He stops and looks around

They are gone. He sees the picture on the floor, picks it up and looks at it, gently lays it on the top of a tree stump and rests his head on it

SCENE 4

Angela, Titus and Miranda are back at home. Miranda is painting over some of the rules. Angela is trying to pull Titus's mask off

Angela Keep still.

Titus Owwwww! You're hurting me.

Angela I'm doing my best.

Titus Your nails are digging into my neck.

Angela What did you do to make it so stuck?

Titus Get it off. I can hardly breathe.

Angela Perhaps some custard might make it more slippery.

Titus We finished the custard last night. On the banana cake.

Angela Of course we did. Miranda, will you help me wrench it off? I think your strength might make the difference. You grab the mask and I'll grab his feet, then on my command we'll pull.

Miranda grabs the mask. Angela grabs his feet

   Have you got a good grip?

Titus Wait wait wait! This sounds a bit drastic. I value my ears, you know.

Angela I'll count down from three.

Titus Hang on! What about olive oil?! What about egg whites?!

Angela Three.

Titus Please.

Angela Two.

Titus Try to be gentle.

Angela One.

Titus I feel dizzy.

Angela *Pull*!!

They pull. Titus yells. The mask comes away. He continues yelling for a few seconds, then checks that all of his facial features are still attached to his head

Titus That didn't hurt as much as I thought it would.

Angela Good. Now, sit down and I'll serve up the kippers.

Titus Kippers?! Oh, wow! Kippers, Miranda!

Miranda What about the lobster claws? You said that if we had fish for breakfast we'd grow claws——

Angela Yes, I'm sorry. We'll paint over that one.
Titus I was wondering what that smoky smell was!
Angela Come and sit down.

Titus and Miranda sit at the table. Angela serves

Kippers for Titus. Kippers for Miranda. Kipper for me.

Angela sits. Titus takes the salt, Miranda the pepper and Angela the vinegar. Angela and Titus glance to Miranda, unsure as to whether to do the condiment ritual. She smiles

Titus Salt!
Miranda Pepper!
Angela Vinegar!

Switch

Titus Pepper!
Miranda Vinegar!
Angela Salt!

Switch

Titus Vinegar!
Miranda Salt!
Angela Pepper! (*She closes her eyes and rests her fingers on her nose*) Thank you for the tasty plate of kippers we're about to eat... Let's just get stuck in, shall we?

They eat. Gradually, unnoticed by them, their hands turn into lobster claws

Titus My head feels like a feather without that mask stuck on it. I hardly slept a wink.
Miranda That's funny, you were snoring like an earthquake.
Titus I do not snore.
Miranda I had to stuff socks in my ears.
Titus At least when I eat I don't make squelching notes.
Angela Before Titus's father died, every day would start with a kipper.

Pause

Miranda Can I give some kipper to Animal?

Angela Why? Don't you like it?
Miranda I just think he might like it.

Angela forces a smile in agreement. Miranda goes to feed Animal

Titus I'm going to start a new painting today. A massive blue guinea pig
   playing a guitar.
Miranda He loves it! He almost bit my hand off!
Angela Dear old Animal.
Miranda That scab is definitely smaller.
Titus And a squirrel on the piano in the background.

Miranda comes back to the table. Pause

Angela What colour paint shall I buy for the walls?
Titus Red. No, indigo. No, orange and black stripes.
Miranda I think you should paint them honey-coloured.

Pause

   Pass the pepper.

Titus passes the pepper, Miranda points at his hand

   Titus! Your hands! They've turned into claws!
Titus Oh my…! So have yours!

Miranda lets out a stifled scream

   Mum?

*Angela slowly lifts her hands to reveal more claws. They stare at each other's
claws, amazed. They turn and look at Animal, who also has claws. They hold
their own claws up to the light and inspect them in a fascinated and
flabbergasted way*

CURTAIN

FURNITURE AND PROPERTY LIST

Further dressing may be added at the director's discretion

ACT I

On stage: ANGELA'S HOUSE:
Beds
Tables. *On one of them*: three plates, three large plastic spoons,
    egg-holding ornament with three eggs
Chairs
Kitchen stuff
Hair brush
Angela's slippers
Gong
Warm cupboard containing dressing-gown
Pot of peas
Sugar bowl with sugar cubes
Cups of tea
Teaspoons
Salt
Pepper
Vinegar
Animal's cage
Biscuit
Carrot
Worm
Writing and painting tools
Washing-up bowl with note "No hiding of toothbrushes" on side
2 mops
2 mackintoshes
Microwave
Household object with note "Don't wear yellow socks."
Milk
Banana
Candle
Matches

Off stage: Palette, paintbrush (**Titus**)
              Toothpaste, sticks, beer, make-up (**Miranda**)
              Bottle of medicine (**Angela**)

Personal: **Titus:** beret

ACT II

SCENE 1

On stage: EDGE OF WOOD:
              Tree stump containing picture frame
              Tree stump containing doll
              Tree stump containing miniature pair of striped pyjamas on hanger,
                 stack of masks, two green apples
              Tree stump containing peculiar rabbit
              Pile of blackened twigs, ash
              Circle of stones and boulders
              Branches
              Grimy black plastic sheet

Off stage: Traffic cone (**Titus**)

Personal: **Miranda:** foil-wrapped biscuit

SCENE 2

On stage: Rock

Personal: **Angela:** rucksack

SCENE 3

On stage: EDGE OF WOOD

SCENE 4

On stage: ANGELA'S HOUSE

Set: Painting tools
              Table set for breakfast
              Kippers in dish

Personal: **Titus:** mask

LIGHTING PLOT

Property fittings required: nil
1 interior / 2 exterior locations

ACT I

To open: Darkness

Cue 1   **Angela's Voice**: "...be careful with the ornaments..."   (Page 1)
            Bring up very slight light on **Titus** *and* **Miranda**

Cue 2   **Miranda** turns light on   (Page 1)
            Snap on general light

Cue 3   **Miranda**: "Didn't I say?"   (Page 15)
            Distant flash of lightning

Cue 4   **Miranda** starts banging plastic spoon on table   (Page 17)
            Closer flash of lightning

Cue 5   **Titus** grabs a mop   (Page 19)
            Closer flash of lightning

Cue 6   **Miranda** begins dancing   (Page 20)
            Closer flash of lightning

Cue 7   **Titus** changes from conducting to dancing   (Page 20)
            Closer flash of lightning

Cue 8   **Miranda** resumes dancing   (Page 20)
            Closer flash of lightning

Cue 9   **Titus** climbs on to table   (Page 20)
            Flash of lightning very nearby

Cue 10   **Angela** screams   (Page 20)
            *Almighty flash of lightning striking house; effect of
            light-bulbs blowing; then dim eclipse-like light*

ACT II, SCENE 1

To open: Twilight and long shadows

No cues

ACT II, SCENE 2

To open: As before

No cues

ACT II, SCENE 3

To open: Darkness

Cue 11   **Titus**: "We're being blown away!"   (Page 29)
              Flashes of lightning revealing **Titus**; *cut suddenly,*
                 bring up weak light

ACT II, SCENE 4

To open: General lighting

No cues

EFFECTS PLOT

ACT I

Cue 1   To open Act I   (Page 1)
Play tape recording of **Angela's Voice** *as script page 1*

Cue 2   **Angela's Voice**: "…no climbing into the refrigerator…"   (Page 1)
Alarm clocks buzz in strange stereo

Cue 3   The children switch off alarms and tape   (Page 1)
Cut alarms and tape

Cue 4   **Titus**: "…to the tips of my whiskers!"   (Page 16)
Distant rumble of thunder

Cue 5   Lightning as **Miranda** starts banging plastic spoon   (Page 17)
Louder rumble of thunder

Cue 6   **Miranda**: "On guard, potato-brained warrior!"   (Page 19)
Louder rumble of thunder and sound of rain outside

Cue 7   **Miranda**: "Who plays records any more?"   (Page 20)
Loud classical music off stage

Cue 8   Lightning as **Miranda** begins dancing   (Page 20)
Louder rumble of thunder

Cue 9   Lightning as **Titus** begins to dance   (Page 20)
Louder rumble of thunder

Cue 10   Lightning as **Miranda** resumes dancing   (Page 20)
Louder rumble of thunder

Cue 11   Lightning as **Titus** climbs on to table   (Page 20)
Very loud rumble of thunder

Cue 12   Lightning as **Angela** screams   (Page 21)
Sound of offstage record player exploding

ACT II

APPENDIX

The house is decorated with the following rules:

General Rules
No squinting at the kitchen floor
No skidding on the kitchen floor
No handstands in the kitchen
No bare feet in the kitchen
No climbing into the refrigerator
No standing on chairs
No standing on tables
No elbows on the table
No juggling with fruit
No wasting juice
No making mixtures
No fiddling with paper clips
Don't stand too near the microwave
Sheets must be washed on Saturdays
Don't lean against the washing machine
Don't breathe against the window
Never open the window before midday
Don't press your face against the window
Don't sniff too much
No imagining of future events
No quacking like ducks
No throwing of knives
No opening sleeping people's eyes
No pillow fights
Hold your breath for 30 seconds at 3.00pm
Cross your legs at 6.19pm
No cheese before bed
No pulling about of other people's faces
No hitting, pinching or scratching
No caterwauling or howling
All singing must be gentle
Only French must be spoken on Tuesday afternoons
No pretending to be caterpillars

No encouraging of cats
Absolutely no kissing of dogs
No setting fire to things
No tramping over the pea patch
Don't stamp in puddles or mud
No jumping in high winds
No sunbathing under tennis rackets
No teetering on curbs or walls
No putting glue on hands then picking it off
Glitter must be used sparingly
No messing with clingfilm
No highlighter pens
No chucking sultanas about
No pretending to be dead or asleep
No chewing of gum whatsoever
No pretending to chew gum
No pretending to smoke
No shouting "penguin" at nuns
The sink must be swilled after use
No fake mice
No giggling at strangers
No spinning around and getting dizzy
Shoes must be polished on Tuesdays
Christmas presents must be opened on Boxing Day
No kneeling on slippers
No nursing poorly birds or bats
Never open Animal's cage
Animal's special diet must be strictly stuck to
No whistling with fingers
No exaggerated sneezes
Scarves must travel twice around the neck
Wipe the bath with the soft green cloth
Wipe the toilet with the harsh red cloth
Itching powder is strictly forbidden
No badges
No boxing or wrestling
Teeth must be flossed on Sunday mornings
No wearing watches round your ankles
No pretending your fingers are guns
No accumulating lolly-sticks
No crunching ice in your mouth
No hoarding of biscuits

Rules for Breakfast
Breakfast must be eaten with a large plastic spoon
Breakfast must consist of peas and only peas
No making up songs about breakfast
No pretending your peas are an army
No pushing peas about your plate
No putting them in pictures, patterns or lines
No speaking on behalf of peas
No banging of plastic spoons
No spilling
No yawning
No salt without pepper
No swallowing without chewing
No flicking

Rules for Mopping
No pretending your mop is a snooker cue
Mackintoshes must be worn
No pretending your mop is a microphone
No shoving mops into other people's faces
One scoop of soap per bucket
One mop per person
No scrapping or skidding
No pretend sword-fighting with mops

A-Z of Rules (On the children's bedroom wall)
Animal's teeth must be brushed bi-annually
Books must be about nice things
Cats must be stroked the right way
Dusting must be done in darkness
Elbows must be scrubbed on Sundays
Faces should not rest on hands
Games must be played sportingly
Hats must be of a single colour
Insects must not be kept in tins
Juice must be drunk through a straw
Karate chopping is not allowed
Light switches must not be used as toys
Monkey noises are not allowed
Nattering at bedtime is forbidden
Old people must be smiled at
Polish your Wellingtons monthly
Quacking is forbidden

Rolling balls about is not allowed
Squealing is not permitted
Tables and chairs must be treated with care
Ulcers must be dabbed with ketchup
Voices should rarely be raised
Worms should not be forced to swim
Xylophone practice must be on Tuesday
Yoghurt must stay in the kitchen
Zebras must never be mentioned

www.ingramcontent.com/pod-product-compliance
Lightning Source LLC
LaVergne TN
LVHW051805080426
835511LV00019B/3411